# THE MINISTRY OF GAIL DUDLEY

Gail Dudley, known for her honest perspective and for her warm and friendly personality, is a committed Christian, focused on preparing believers for ministry. Gail is a true servant of God and one who finds tremendous joy in helping others to become "Ministry-Minded, Ministry-Equipped, Ministry-Motivated, and Ministry-Engaged."

Gail is an ordained pastor and serves alongside her husband in Columbus while working on a Master's degree in Spiritual Formation from Ashland Theological Seminary. Gail serves faithfully as a partner in ministry with Common Grounds Ministries and Equipping Center, responsible for pastoral leadership, facilitating discipleship bible studies, giving guidance to the many expressions of congregational ministry, and overseeing the organization of multiple outreach efforts around the greater Columbus area. Gail is also the visionary of Ministry in Motion Ministry, is committed to delivering Christian teachings, prayer journeys, and conferences for women and girls, and the host of When You Don't Know What To Do women's conference that ministers to the whole person.

Gail has a great desire to engage the growing needs of communities by encouraging creative partnerships between municipal, business, nonprofit and neighborhood resources, and has a passion for social and racial justice, and development of women leaders. Gail is an accomplished conference and workshop speaker who has been privileged to present the Gospel in Canada, England, South Africa, Zimbabwe, Israel, and both Berlin and Herrnhut, Germany, equipping and motivating women around the world to walk boldly into their promised future. On top of all of that, Gail is a publisher serving authors internationally. She is the author of ten books and many other training resources and is the co-founder for READY Publication, an edgy, different, and content-rich quarterly magazine where she works alongside of her daughter.

Gail is married to Dr. Kevin Dudley and the loving mother of Alexander and Dominiq. The calling that God has placed upon Gail's life will touch you as you experience her heart and her spirit filled life-changing messages.

Copyright © 2019 by Gail Dudley

Prayer in Motion
by Gail Dudley
www.GailDudley.com

Printed in the United States of America

ISBN: 978-1-7336986-9-6

All rights reserved. No part of this document may be reproduced or transmitted in any form, by any means (electronic, photocopying, recording, or otherwise) without the written permission of the author.

Unless otherwise indicated, Bible quotations are taken from the Holy Bible, New International Version®, NIV®. Copyright ©1973, 1978, 1984, 2011 by Biblica, Inc.® Used by permission. All rights reserved worldwide.

Scripture marked ESV is taken from the Holy Bible, English Standard Version. ESV® Text Edition: 2016. Copyright © 2001 by Crossway Bibles, a publishing ministry of Good News Publishers.

Scripture marked KJV is taken from the King James Version. Public domain.

Scripture marked NKJV is taken from the New King James Version®. Copyright © 1982 by Thomas Nelson. Used by permission. All rights reserved.

Scripture marked (NLT) is taken from the New Living Translation. Copyright © 1996, 2004, 2015 by Tyndale House Foundation. Used by permission of Tyndale House Publishers, Inc., Carol Stream, Illinois 60188. All rights reserved.

Published by:
Gail Dudley, READY Media LLC
www.READYPublication.com

Editor:
Tam Jernigan

Cover by:
Dominiq Dudley

Interior design by:
Amber Mabry, A Paynes Designs
(www.apaynesdesigns.com)

# INTRODUCTION

> This is not a book that will read like a story. It is a prayer manual. It's a tool that you can use to guide you along your prayer journey. Pray long prayers? Short prayers? Lift up the name of Jesus when you are exhausted? This manual is for you. Hosting a prayer summit, organizing prayer walks, or a missionary prayer journey? This manual is for you.

I pause long enough to take in the beauty of God's hands upon my life and the calling He has placed within me. I will not take lightly or gloss over the times in my life when I have prayed during times of difficulty, exhaustion, frustration, chaos, and challenges. I have been in the space of trying to pray while learning of the death of love ones. Health scares. Financial lack. Relationships. Business uncertainty. Ministry. Questions. Doubts. Life. Yet, even in those times, I can truly say that I have witnessed God's hand more powerfully upon me in those seasons which turned into watching Him beautifully paint a picture of my life as in a mirrored reflection of Him.

God has led me to share my journey with those of you who are seeking to pray deeper, especially in times when you don't want to pray in this prayer manual Prayer in Motion. I'll begin with a story that took place during a Sunday morning in the spring of 2019. To be transparent let me share that I was a mess. I'd accepted my calling to a ministry of prayer several years ago, but I was in a season that I did not feel like praying, did not want to pray, and was mad at God for continuing to use me in a ministry of prayer. Every time I yelled, "I quit" He would send someone to me to ask me to pray for their crisis. I would pray and learn their prayers were answered while the prayers I prayed for myself went unanswered, ignored, dismissed, and forgotten until…

On a Sunday morning, I stood in the sanctuary of a church feeling depleted and frustrated. I didn't want to be there. I would have rather been at home sitting on my patio enjoying me time. God, however, had another plan. He needed me to be seen by a woman who knew me. She walked up to me with these life-giving words. "Pastor Gail, prayer is your superpower. Just pray. That's what you do." She knew I'd had a somewhat challenging year. I now call it my year of stretching.

## IT'S FUNNY THAT I WRITE AND RELEASE THIS BOOK AT THE END OF THE YEAR 2019, WHICH HAS BEEN AN INTERESTING YEAR FOR ME.

In February, God gave me a vision to launch a women's conference after fifteen years of not hosting one. During the early morning of, February 19, 2019 God awakened me to pen the details of everything He was calling me to do in this season. That morning, #WhenYouDontKnowWhatToDo Conference was placed in my womb. One thing was certain, God desires to include His daughters of every race, stage, age, nationality, demographic, economic status, worldview, educational level, and status, which defined *The Call*: We desire to build and create a conference experience where God speaks, and women receive and respond. And, *The Vision*: Implementing a conference blueprint from God of women coming together regardless of race, age, nationality, demographics, social economic status, language, educational level, and disability.

God was speaking to me and I pressed forward even during some of the most intense times of my life. It would have been easy for me to abort the mission, yet I continued to move in the direction God was calling me. Over and over again I heard from women and girls who stated, "I don't know what to do." I could see all of the pieces coming together and the more clarity God would give me the more the enemy would try to distract me. "The enemy comes to steal, kill, and destroy, but Jesus came to bring life more abundantly." Yes, that particular scripture from John 10:10 was etched in my mind. Every time I would consider throwing in the towel, I would hear those words from John 10:10.

I cannot explain it, but the enemy was attacking me daily. The moment I would get some strength another blow would come from another direction. I didn't know what to do, but pray. I had to tap into my superpower and seek the face of the Lord, even when I didn't feel like it. Hear me, I wanted to quit! I could not understand why I was being hit so hard over and over again. The list is too long to list here, but you name it, it was happening to me. Death of loved one, Medical challenges. Financial Debt. Health issue with family members. Lies being spewed. Business challenges. Lack of sleep. Fear. Anxiety. I was ready to walk away from everything…straight out of the door never to return. Why was the enemy coming at me at this pace and this level? I don't know, but I found strength to call out the name of Jesus and hold onto His unchanging hand. I kept telling myself that, "I am victorious!" If you can picture someone with their sleeves rolled up climbing out of a pit pulling down the dirt and as a hand would cup the dirt and pull it down, their foot was using that pulled dirt to climb a little higher…that was me! I made a decision to come out of the pit and know that Jesus is King and I am a child of the Most High. Once I made it up in my mind that I am more than a conqueror of Jesus I felt the atmosphere shift.

# ON THE MORNING OF, SUNDAY, JUNE 23, 2019,

6:33 am to be exact, I was sitting in my car at Hoover Dam. The Holy Spirit had awakened me to shower, get dressed, and drive to that very spot. When I arrived, I experienced one of those audible times when I heard the Lord ask, *"What do you see?"*

I pulled out my journal and penned these words, *"What Do I See?"*

*Journal entry – Sunday, June 23, 19 6:37 am*

> What Do I See?
>
> God's sun reflected on the water
> I see trees softly blowing
> I see small ripples throughout a body of water
>
> I see His beauty and I sense God's peace
> It's calming!
>
> This is the day the Lord has made, Let us rejoice and be glad (Psalm 34:1)
>
> I see the manifestation of God's glory.
>
> Psalm 34:4 "I sought the Lord, and he answered me; he delivered me from all of my fears."
>
> Vs. 10 "The lions may grow weak and hungry, but those who seek the Lord lack no good thing."
>
> Vs. 12 – 14 "Whoever of you loves life and desire to see many good days, keep your tongue from evil and your lips from speaking lies. Turn from evil and do good, seek peace and pursue it."
>
> Psalm 35:28
> "My tongue will speak of your righteousness and of your praises all day long. "
>
> God led me to Acts 9:18 which says, "Immediately, something like scales fell from Saul's eyes, and he could see again. He got up and was baptized,"
>
> I can see. Scales are falling from my eyes. I'm excited.
>
> I HAVE MY ASSIGNMENT !
>
> I had to see it before God could release it!
>
> NOTE: A shift took place at 7:59 am – going into 8:00 am (new beginning).
>
> *Journal entry ended.*

Something happened that morning. I started getting my strength back. I felt the presence of the Lord upon me. There was a fresh anointing. I could see supernaturally. I began praying with more intimacy. I had put my prayer in motion.

The devil was mad.
He came at me with a force greater than earlier in the year.

The conference I mentioned earlier in the introduction was set to launch on, my 54th birthday. July 19, 2019 to be exact. Well, one week before on a Friday evening while eating, I felt my tongue enlarge. Soon thereafter I could barely breathe. Within a few moments my windpipe was almost closed. While sitting in Urgent Care around the corner from my home, 911 was dispatched and my oxygen was dropping. It had hit below fifty percent. Oxygen mask, Epi-pens injected and off to the nearest hospital I went traveling by ambulance. That night I was admitted into the hospital. Confused. Concerned. Crying. However, communicating. Something I could not do a few hours earlier. Unsure what was going on, one thing I knew was that it was too late to quit now.

The conference was before me. God had called me to it.
Surely His plan was set to launch.

*Journal entry – July 19, 2019*

> #WhenYouDontKnowWhatToDo conference launch day.
>
> It's been a fight since the early morning in February you deposited this vision on the inside of me. Today is the day. Lord have Your way.
>
> *Journal entry ended.*

There's so much I have not shared with you from February 19 up to October 1, 2019. Just know it has been a journey. I did not quit. Having regular conversations with God kept me. I won't lie and say that everything has been perfect since July. It has not. However, I am praying. I am crying out to God. I am hearing the voice of God. I am discerning and seeing at a deeper level since the scales have been removed from my eyes and I have set my prayer in motion.

No turning back now. Today as you hold this prayer manual in your hands, I am asking you to join me on this intentional prayer movement.

Haven't you noticed all of the chaos and heard all of the noise? Are you witnessing a greater divide in the world? Are you witnessing the confusion? Do you feel things intensifying? God said in his word, "*If my people, which are called by my name, shall humble themselves, and pray, and seek my face, and turn from their wicked ways; then will I hear from heaven, and will forgive their sin, and will heal their land.*" 2 Chronicles 7:14 KJV

I have set my prayer in motion. I'm ready. Are you ready? Let's go!

# LAYING THE FOUNDATION

## YOU HOLD IN YOUR HANDS THIS PRAYER MANUAL. USE THIS AS A WEAPON.

My hope is that you carry this from room to room in your home, have it in your car to pull out while you are in stopped traffic, throw it in your tote bag, carry it with you on the plane, riding in a train, or have it with you while you are walking on the treadmill. The hope is that you can easily access this magazine like prayer manual whenever you need.

**This manual is divided into three sections.**

1. Cry Out to God
2. Hearing the Voice of God
3. Discernment…Seeing

Plus 31-Days of Prayer, prayer positions, and other prayer resources.

Each section will include prompters, scriptures, and some instructions.

*Know this…*
**There is power in what you say.**

"The tongue has the power of life and death, and those who love it will eat its fruit." Proverbs 18:21 NIV

**Watch what you say. Do not say things that are limiting or negative.**

Psalm 19:14 "May the words of my mouth and the meditation of my heart be pleasing in your sight, O Lord, my Rock and my Redeemer."

## PRAYER:

In the name of Jesus, I speak life to each reader and student of prayer. I pray your guidance, obedience, direction, a fresh anointment, an increase in your discernment, encouragement, boldness, and opportunities to minister and to pray alongside and with others as the Spirit of the Lord leads. I pray your life to be strengthened by the power of the Holy Spirit. I pray the blood of Jesus upon and within your life. I pray that you are stretched in an unusual way and that your faith is strengthened in, Christ. I pray your life will overflow with abundance of the grace of the Lord. I pray the many gifts God has placed on the inside of you are stirred to move you to another level in Him during this new season in your life. I declare and decree that you will be a lender and not a borrower in the name of Jesus. I declare that you are blessed in the city and you are blessed in the field. I pray that you will bear much fruit in all that you put your hands too. I speak abundance, knowledge, and wisdom. I pray your prosperity in the Word of the Lord. I pray for ministry resources and thank You in advance for manifesting Your Word and Your presence in our lives according to 3 John 2; "Beloved, I wish above all things that thou mayest prosper and be in health, even as thy soul prospereth."

In the mighty and precious—most powerful name of Jesus, AMEN!

# CRY OUT TO GOD

PRAYER IN MOTION

> "**CALL TO ME** and I will answer you and tell you great and unsearchable things you do not know."
>
> Jeremiah 33:3 NIV

# SECTION 1

# CRY OUT TO GOD

# God is saying, "Call to me."

call out my name.

- This is about having an intimate relationship with God. He is saying to us, "Call out my name." Yes, go ahead and cry out to God. Lament! He can handle it. Abba Father, help me! Lord, draw me from the pit. Jesus, I'm tired. Regardless if you are exhausted, afraid, asking questions, joyous, confused, praising or worshiping, God is telling us to call out His name.

petition me.

- Google defines petition as to appealing to authority with respect to a particular cause.
- God is saying, "Appear to me. What is your cause?"
- God is inviting us to share with Him.

seek me.

God is saying, "Look for Me." Look for God in everything you do. Seek His handprint and sense His presence. Even in the most difficult and challenging situations, God is there. Seek Him. The Bible says, "Seek the LORD while you can find him. Call on him now while he is near." (Isaiah 55:6 NLT)

All throughout the Bible God is revealing to us how He may be found. He is giving us instructions over and over again. The question is, are we listening? Do we know His voice? God is also saying…

spend time with me.

- Want to know God's voice? Spend time with Him. (read more in the next section 'Hearing the Voice of God')
- Wake up early
- Stay up later and spend time with God
- Turn off the radio while driving and talk to God
- Pray as you wash dishes, cook, clean the kitchen, or while washing and folding clothes. There are so many opportunities to spend time with God.

**GRAB A PEN AND SOME PAPER** and jot down all the times throughout your day that you can spend time with God and start spending time with Him today.

For example, my list includes:

- Quiet time in the bathroom. *(yes, that place)*
- While taking a shower. Some people sing. I talk to God.
- Walking around my home. This is where I also take back territory the enemy may have been trying to take hold of.
- Making the bed. I pray for a hedge of protection and ask God to give us sweet rest.
- Sitting on the patio. I look out at the beauty of God (trees, grass, birds, etc.) and begin to thank God.
- Driving. As I pass an accident, I pray for whoever may be involved and their friends and family, and any physicians if they need medical attention. I pray for homes as I drive past them and I also pray for businesses.
- While grocery shopping. I'm praying for the people that I pass and the workers. Yes, I even pray for great prices.

These are just some ideas. The main point I want to make is the importance of spending time with the Lord.

God is also saying, *"Know me. Rest in me. Walk with me."*

know me.

- When you spend time with God, you begin to know Him. This isn't any different than when you make new relationships with your friends, family, co-workers, and spouse.
- You can learn everything you need to know about Jesus by reading and studying the Bible.

rest in me.
- Yes. Rest!
- "Be still and know…" (Psalm 46:10)

**walk with me.**
- Let's talk about exercise. That's one way of getting it in. Walk with God.

When I take a walk throughout the neighborhood, I am praying, spending time with God, and praying for every home I pass. I will never forget walking past a home and felt the call to stop and pray. I could not leave that spot. I remember praying more intensely. After five minutes or so I felt the release to move on. Later that day, while chatting with my neighbor, she asked me to pray for a family in our neighborhood that was dealing with some major health issues, stress, and job loss. I have no idea if the family lived in the home I was led to stop and pray, but it confirmed for me that we must be obedient to God's instructions as we walk with Him.

God's response? He says, "Call to me and I will answer you…" #Relationship

**Pause for a moment and evaluate your relationship with Jesus.**
Think about your close relationships, both family and friends. Consider your co-workers, neighbors, etc.

> Now read Genesis 24:1-21. Here you will find an example of a relationship that grew over time. Yes, it takes time to build relationships.
>
> Verse 11 in Genesis 24 says, "He had the camels kneel down near the well outside of the town; it was toward evening, the time the women go out to draw water."
>
> Verse 12 says, "Then he prayed, "O Lord, God of my master Abraham, give me success today and show kindness to my master Abraham."

Notice the prayer that he prayed wasn't just for him. It included others. It included his master Abraham, and Abraham's son and the woman. This relationship started between Abraham and his chief servant.

## Genesis 24:1-21 NIV

Abraham was now very old, and the Lord had blessed him in every way. 2 He said to the senior servant in his household, the one in charge of all that he had, "Put your hand under my thigh. 3 I want you to swear by the Lord, the God of heaven and the God of earth, that you will not get a wife for my son from the daughters of the Canaanites, among whom I am living, 4 but will go to my country and my own relatives and get a wife for my son Isaac."

5 The servant asked him, "What if the woman is unwilling to come back with me to this land? Shall I then take your son back to the country you came from?"

6 "Make sure that you do not take my son back there," Abraham said. 7 "The Lord, the God of heaven, who brought me out of my father's household and my native land and who spoke to me and promised me on oath, saying, 'To your offspring[a] I will give this land'—he will send his angel before you so that you can get a wife for my son from there. 8 If the woman is unwilling to come back with you, then you will be released from this oath of mine. Only do not take my son back there." 9 So the servant put his hand under the thigh of his master Abraham and swore an oath to him concerning this matter.

10 Then the servant left, taking with him ten of his master's camels loaded with all kinds of good things from his master. He set out for Aram Naharaim[b] and made his way to the town of Nahor. 11 He had the camels kneel down near the well outside the town; it was toward evening, the time the women go out to draw water.

12 Then he prayed, "Lord, God of my master Abraham, make me successful today, and show kindness to my master Abraham. 13 See, I am standing beside this spring, and the daughters of the townspeople are coming out to draw water. 14 May it be that when I say to a young woman, 'Please let down your jar that I may have a drink,' and she says, 'Drink, and I'll water your camels too'—let her be the one you have chosen for your servant Isaac. By this I will know that you have shown kindness to my master."

15 Before he had finished praying, Rebekah came out with her jar on her shoulder. She was the daughter of Bethuel son of Milkah, who was the wife of Abraham's brother Nahor. 16 The woman was very beautiful, a virgin; no man had ever slept with her. She went down to the spring, filled her jar and came up again.

17 The servant hurried to meet her and said, "Please give me a little water from your jar."

18 "Drink, my lord," she said, and quickly lowered the jar to her hands and gave him a drink.

19 After she had given him a drink, she said, "I'll draw water for your camels too, until they have had enough to drink." 20 So she quickly emptied her jar into the trough, ran back to the well to draw more water, and drew enough for all his camels. 21 Without saying a word, the man watched her closely to learn whether or not the Lord had made his journey successful.

Notice the chief servant's relationship with God.

There had to have been a solid relationship for the chief servant to pray this prayer and for God to answer before he had finished praying.

# Let's look *closely* at what he prayed.

1) He prayed, "O Lord, God of my master Abraham." We know God answered his prayer BEFORE he had finished praying, but notice how he prayed, "God of my master Abraham." Look back at the verse one and two. Abraham was old and well advanced in years. The Lord had truly blessed Abraham.

If you consider Abraham's life journey, you will know he was obedient to God in every way. Look at Isaac – God called Abraham to sacrifice his only son Isaac. Abraham was obedient. He also knew his God. If you read Genesis 22:5 it reads, "He said to his servants, "Stay here with the donkey while I and the boy go over there. We will worship and then WE will come back to you. "

Then again as Abraham took wood for the offering and carried the knife and fire, his own son raised the questions, "Father?" "The fire and wood are here, but where is the lamb for the burnt offering?" (vs 7)

Read Abraham's reply slowly and carefully. He said, "God himself will provide the lamb for the burnt offering my son."

When they had arrived to build the altar, Abraham laid his son Isaac on the top of the wood ready to take his knife and slay his own, but the angel of the Lord yelled out, "Do not lay a hand on the boy."

**Question:** *Do you extend your prayers to reach others in your circle of influence and beyond? Why or why not?* Depending upon your answer, take time to pray and ask God to show you how to include others into your prayers. For example. When I pray for finances, I ask God to bless His children who are in debt due to medical bills to experience debt cancellation. Not only am I praying for me, but I am now praying for everyone who is in debt due to medical bills. It's altering your prayers to include more than just you and your immediate need or circumstance. When we begin putting our prayers in motion that includes others, everyone benefits including you.

## Let's continue to look at relationships.

Genesis 12:1-4
"The Lord had said to Abram, "Leave your country, your people and your father's household and go to the land I will show you."

Abram goes without question.
In Genesis 15:1 the Lord came to Abram in a vision saying, "Do not be afraid, Abram. I am your shield, your very great reward."

In chapter 17 the Lord appeared to Abram when he was ninety-nine years old and said, "I am God Almighty, walk before me and be blameless. I will confirm my covenant between me and you and will greatly increase your numbers."

2) Give me success today.

Right now. Before the day is over.

3) Show kindness to my master Abraham
4) See, I am standing…

- Look at me, Lord
- See what I am doing
- Know my position.

5) May it be…

He gives specifics. This is not a general prayer. He gives details.

- When I say
- …to a girl
- …"Let down your jar that I may have a drink
- She says, "Drink, and I'll water your camels too"
- Let that be the one.

**STOP:** Please read Genesis 24:11 again. "He (the chief servant) had the camels kneel down near the well OUTSIDE of the town…"

If I were in front of you, I would say, "Okay, let's read the following scriptures out loud."

"Before he had finished praying, Rebekah came out with her jar on her shoulder." (Genesis 24:15)

The answer.

> Verse 17: The servant says, "Please give me a little water from your jar."
> Verse 18: "Drink my lord."
> Verse 19: "I'll draw water for your camels too…"

Remember, the chief servant was standing and praying beside the spring without any camels beside him.

Don't miss this! As I glee with excitement because typing these words in this manual has created a renewed smile on my face. Yes, I get excited when God manifests his glory right in front of me.

## CALL TO ME. Pray to me.
## Have a relationship with Me so you may hear His voice.

Don't just hear it.

Live into it.

Live it.

Take action when He speaks.

Jeremiah 29:12-13

"Then you will call upon me and come and pray to me, and I will listen to you. You will seek me and find me when you seek me with all your heart."

Most times we stop after reading or reciting, Jeremiah 29:11, but you can see in verses twelve and thirteen that there's more to that story. It starts with a very powerful word. Then. Let's put that into practice.

"For I know the plans I have for you," declares the Lord, "plans to prosper you and not to harm you, plans to give you hope and a future." (Jeremiah 29:11) THEN…(Jeremiah 29:12-13). Learn to read the verses to the scriptures before and after the one you land on in order to glean the full story.

## MEMORY VERSES

Jeremiah 33:3 NIV

"Call to me and I will answer you and tell you great and unsearchable things you do not know."

Psalm 5:1-3

"Give ear to my words, O Lord, consider my sighing. Listen to my cry for help, my King and my God, for to you I pray. In the morning, O Lord, you hear my voice; in the morning I lay my request before you and wait in expectation." NIV

Psalm 6:9

"The Lord has heard my cry for mercy; the Lord accepts my prayer." NIV

Psalm 17:1-2

"Hear, O Lord, my righteous plea; listen to my cry. Give ear to my prayer—it does not rise from deceitful lips. May my vindication come from you; may your eyes see what is right." NIV

Psalm 86:6-7 NIV

"Hear my prayer, Lord; listen to my cry for mercy. 7 When I am in distress, I call to you, because you answer me."

# REMEMBER BLIND BARTIMAEUS

[46] Then they came to Jericho. As Jesus and his disciples, together with a large crowd, were leaving the city, a blind man, Bartimaeus (which means "son of Timaeus"), was sitting by the roadside begging. [47] When he heard that it was Jesus of Nazareth, he began to shout, "Jesus, Son of David, have mercy on me!" [48] Many rebuked him and told him to be quiet, but he shouted all the more, "Son of David, have mercy on me!" [49] Jesus stopped and said, "Call him." So they called to the blind man, "Cheer up! On your feet! He's calling you." [50] Throwing his cloak aside, he jumped to his feet and came to Jesus. [51] "What do you want me to do for you?" Jesus asked him. The blind man said, "Rabbi, I want to see." [52] "Go," said Jesus, "your faith has healed you." Immediately he received his sight and followed Jesus along the road. [Mark 10:46-52 NIV]

What did he do? He cried out and received the attention of Jesus even when Jesus' boys tried to silence him.

Who's trying to silence you? Most times, we silence ourselves based upon bad theology. Scripture after scripture, God is calling us to cry out.

Merriam-Webster defines cry out to mean, 1: to make a loud sound because of pain, fear, surprise, etc. She *cried out* in pain. 2: to speak in a loud voice: to say something loudly or from a distance

Set your prayer in motion. It's time to cry out!

PRAYER IN MOTION

# HEARING THE VOICE OF GOD

"HE will answer our prayers.

The question becomes,
Do you know His Voice?"

Jeremiah 33:3 NIV

# SECTION 2

# *HEARING THE VOICE OF GOD*

As we covered in section one, looking at Jeremiah 33:3, we see that God will not only hear our prayers, but He will answer our prayers. The question becomes, "*Do you know His voice?*"

Knowing His voice comes with spending time with God. So often we think we will receive an audible response from God. No. Most times He speaks through our reading of the Bible. Sometimes He speaks through a confirm word from others, which means He spoke to you first. Until we have spent time with God, we may miss His voice speaking to us.

Turn off the noise. Do you know that we can drown Jesus out by playing music? We think music gets us in the mood to hear from Him. Not always. We could be blocking hearing His still small voice.

Exercise. Find a place and sit quietly for five minutes. After you have sat in a time of silence write down everything that happened. Did you think about all you have to do? Did you notice dust?

Let's do this exercise once more, but this time practicing Lectio Divina. You will need your Bible for this exercise this time around. If possible please use a hardcopy of the Bible and not your electronic device.

**Lectio Divina** *defined*: "(Latin for "Divine Reading") is a traditional monastic practice of scriptural reading, meditation and prayer intended to promote communion with God and to increase the knowledge of God's word. It does not treat scripture as texts to be studied, but as the living word."

**There are 5 Steps:**

1. **Reading** ~ Read a passage of Scripture slowly and softly.
2. **Prayer** ~ Engage in a personal conversation with God.
3. **Peaceful, Meditation** ~ Thinking deeply but be at peace.
4. **Submit** ~ Rest in the presence of God.
5. **Action** ~ Live into it. Take action when God speaks.

> You can engage in this practice using any Scripture, but in this prayer manual we will use John 14:9-14.

⁹ Jesus answered: "Don't you know me, Philip, even after I have been among you such a long time? Anyone who has seen me has seen the Father. How can you say, 'Show us the Father'? ¹⁰ Don't you believe that I am in the Father, and that the Father is in me? The words I say to you I do not speak on my own authority. Rather, it is the Father, living in me, who is doing his work. ¹¹ Believe me when I say that I am in the Father and the Father is in me; or at least believe on the evidence of the works themselves. ¹² Very truly I tell you, whoever believes in me will do the works I have been doing, and they will do even greater things than these, because I am going to the Father. ¹³ And I will do whatever you ask in my name, so that the Father may be glorified in the Son. ¹⁴ You may ask me for anything in my name, and I will do it." John 14:9-14

1. First reading – listen to the passage. Read aloud and hear yourself speak.

2. Second reading – This time read slowly. Using your journal, write down one word or phrase that stands out to you.

3. Third reading – This time read even more slowly. Pause at each comma and period. Using your journal, write down what is Jesus speaking to you through that word or phrase.

4. Fourth reading – Read through the passage of scripture once more. Answer the questions, "What is Jesus inviting me into? How is Jesus leading me?"

Reading through a passage of scriptures four times should create new meaning in the words you are reading. Do you feel a difference? Do you see a manifestation of prayer from this exercise? Can you hear God speaking?

## Distractions…

Unless you control or get rid of the distractions in your life – they may prevent you from hearing the voice of God.

There is a reality of God's people spending their lives with wishful thinking and making decisions based on "Their" knowledge – "Their" understanding – "Their" experiences. Here is an invitation to submit to God and to hear His voice.

God wants to show us – Himself (Phil. 3:7-8)

- vs. 8 "…of knowing Christ Jesus my Lord…"
  In order to hear the voice of God we must "Know" God – not knowing about God BUT to "Know" God – so in tune and in touch; our heartbeat is with His.

Antithesis (The Problem): I can't hear God – I don't know if it is God speaking – Whose voice is who…"

---

Let's look at John 10:3-10

John 10:3-10 NIV "The watchman opens the gate for him, and the sheep listen to his voice. He calls his own sheep by name and leads them out. When he has brought out all of his own, he goes on ahead of them, and his sheep follow him because they know his voice. But they will never follow a stranger; in fact, they will run away from him because they do not recognize a stranger's voice." Jesus used this figure of speech, but they did not understand what he was telling them. Therefore, Jesus said again, "I tell you the truth, I am the gate for the sheep. All who ever came before me were thieves and robbers, but the sheep did not listen to them. I am the gate; whoever enters through me will be saved. He will come in and go out, and find pasture. The thief comes only to steal and kill and destroy; I have come that they may have life, and have it to the full."

God's sheep know His voice. Parents know their children's voice. I know my parents voice. Why?

Because parents spend time with their children and children spend time with their parents. We do not have to see them to know their voice. Once we spend time with God and in His word, we will know His voice.

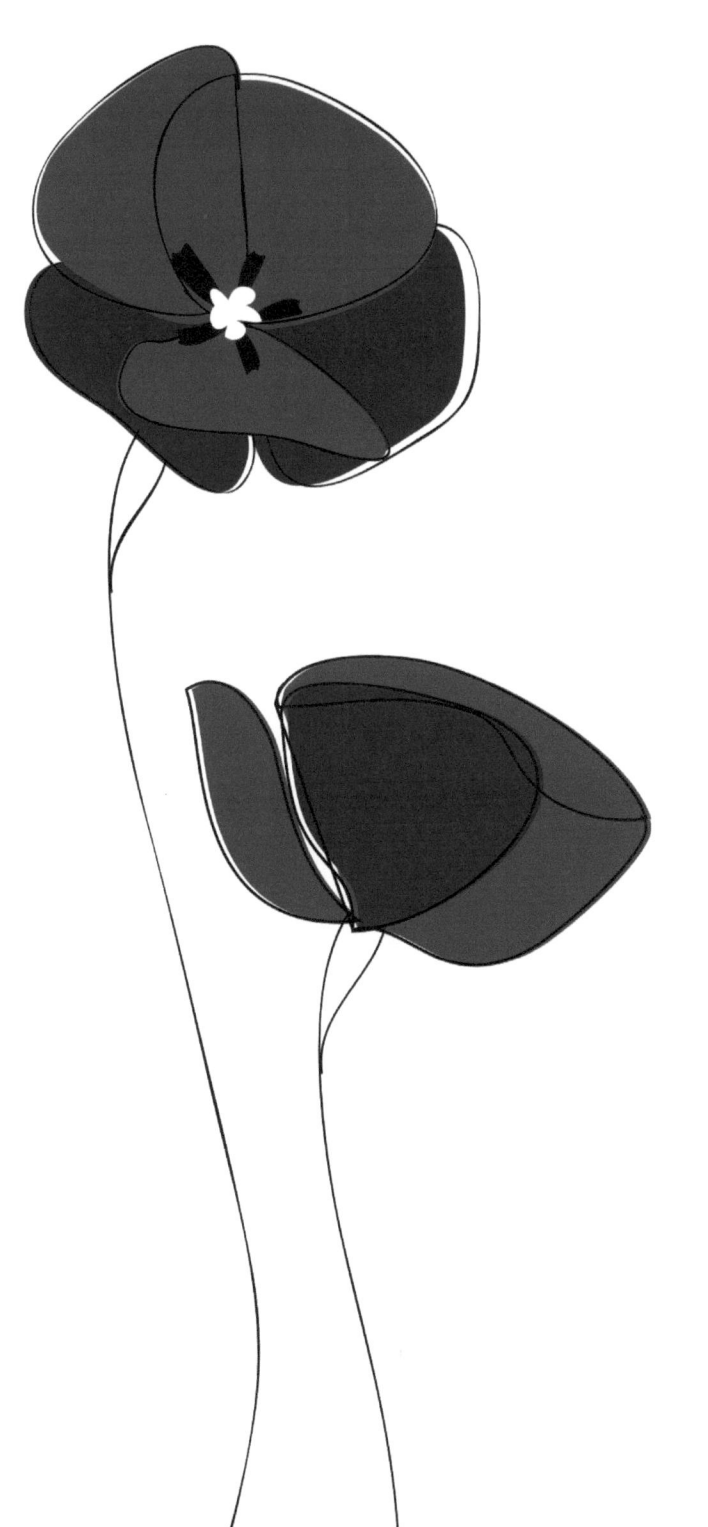

PRAYER IN MOTION

# SPIRITUAL DISCERNMENT AND SEEING

# Question: Have you found it difficult to see lately?

# SECTION 3

> believe on the evidence of the miracles themselves. ¹²I tell you the truth, anyone who has faith in me will do what I have been doing. He will do even greater things than these, because I am going to the Father. ¹³And I will do whatever you ask in my name, so that the Son may bring glory to the Father. ¹⁴You may ask me for anything in my name, and I will do it.

## *SPIRITUAL DISCERNMENT ...SEEING*

*¹⁵ But the Lord said to Ananias, "Go! This man is my chosen instrument to proclaim my name to the Gentiles and their kings and to the people of Israel. ¹⁶ I will show him how much he must suffer for my name." ¹⁷ Then Ananias went to the house and entered it. Placing his hands on Saul, he said, "Brother Saul, the Lord—Jesus, who appeared to you on the road as you were coming here—has sent me so that you may see again and be filled with the Holy Spirit." 18 Immediately, something like scales fell from Saul's eyes, and he could see again. He got up and was baptized, 19 and after taking some food, he regained his strength.* Acts 9:15-19

---

Have you found it difficult to see? Trouble seeing the stress in your household? Trouble seeing someone close to you crying out for help? Trouble seeing what God may be specifically speaking to you in this season? Trouble seeing the truth?

Take a moment and place your hands over your eyes and pray, "God, remove the scales from my eyes so that I may see." Remove your hands from your eyes. What do you see?

Some of us have lost our strength along the way. We have warred for so long that we are tired. We have fought. We have experienced sleepless nights. We have been in a time of spiritual warfare, on the frontlines alone.

"God, remove the scales from our eyes so that we can see."

Now that we can see, get up, take some food, and allow the Lord to work on your behalf. Implement self-care and regain the Lord's strength.

We cannot go nonstop praying and fasting alone. We must take time to rest and see the salvation of the Lord. It is not selfish to go to the spa, have a girl's night out, go to lunch by yourself and enjoy time away. Go to the movies. Walk the park and listen to the birds chirping, watch the trees blow, and sit down on the park bench and be still. Slow the racing of your mind. Unclutter. If you are a male reading this prayer manual, have a men's night out. Enjoy date night with your significant other.

I have spent the day and sometimes an entire weekend sitting in my pajamas watching old black and white movies, old dramas, or sitting with a blanket reading a book that is not the Bible. It's okay. We do not have to be super holy.

> **IF YOU DO NOT TAKE TIME TO REST**, the enemy is coming for you in your weakest moment. Yes, you will still be victorious, but you'll be tired, frustrated and ready to quickly throw in the towel. Pace yourself on your prayer journey. What does your prayer life feel like to you? Is it labor intensive – just trying to make it work and get to the end or is it free.

## 2 Peter 1:5-9 NKJV

⁵ But also for this very reason, giving all diligence, add to your faith virtue, to virtue knowledge, ⁶ to knowledge self-control, to self-control perseverance, to perseverance godliness, ⁷ to godliness brotherly kindness, and to brotherly kindness love. ⁸ For if these things are yours and abound, you will be neither barren nor unfruitful in the knowledge of our Lord Jesus Christ. ⁹ For he who lacks these things is shortsighted, even to blindness, and has forgotten that he was cleansed from his old sins.

### Let's break this down word for word.

- "Faith" Faith is complete trust or confidence in someone or something. That's having faith in God.

- We add to our faith "Virtue." Virtue is having a behavior showing high moral standards. Stop playing low. Stop thinking small. Stop living as if you can't. Start living with higher standards.

- Then we add to virtue "Knowledge." Knowledge means facts, information, skills we acquire through our experience. It's saying, "I have been there and done that and based upon facts and information I CAN DO ALL THINGS THROUGH CHRIST WHO STRENGTHENS ME!"

- Then we add to knowledge "Self-Control." Self-Control is the ability to control oneself, in particular one's emotions and desires or the expression of them in one's behavior, especially in difficult situations. NEVER LET THEM SEE YOU SWEAT!

- Then we add to self-control "Perseverance!" Perseverance is having steadfastness in doing something despite difficulty or delay in achieving success. The Bible tells us in Philippians 3 "But this one thing I do. Forgetting those things which are behind, and reaching forth unto those things which are before, I press toward the mark for the prize of the high calling of God in Christ Jesus."

- Then we add to perseverance "godliness." Then we add to godliness "kindness."

  This is not the time to seek validation from others. We must lean into who God says we are and be obedient to His instructions. Time out for hiding behind false narratives for fear of someone questioning what we have discerned or seen in the spirit.

  We must learn when to speak and when to pray. There's a difference.

## Spiritual Gifting of discernment:

A Spiritual gift is given to each of us so we can help each other. [8] To one person the Spirit gives the ability to give wise advice[a]; to another the same Spirit gives a message of special knowledge. [b] [9] The same Spirit gives great faith to another, and to someone else the one Spirit gives the gift of healing. [10] He gives one person the power to perform miracles, and another the ability to prophesy. He gives someone else the ability to discern whether a message is from the Spirit of God or from another spirit. Still another person is given the ability to speak in unknown languages,[c] while another is given the ability to interpret what is being said. [11] It is the one and only Spirit who distributes all these gifts. He alone decides which gift each person should have. [1 Corinthians 12:7-11 NLT]

## Operating in the spirit of discernment:

- Pray. May the eyes of my understanding be opened. It is important to pay particular attention to those things God has allowed you to see with your eyes. Do not read into what someone else has shared with you or try to project onto you what they believe. That person may be operating in their own strength based upon a history with someone, a church, or an organization and not be operating with a spirit of discernment. As mentioned in section one of this prayer manual, be sure to call out to God. He will answer you. In doing so, remember to study His word and spend time with Him so that you will know it is He who is speaking and showing you things to pray for or He may instruct you to share.

- Deal with any personal offenses and unforgiveness. This is very important. If you do not deal with your own stuff, your ability to hear and discern will be interrupted by your flesh.

    Three of the greatest hindrances are:

    - Unbelief
    - Unforgiveness
    - Unconfessed Sin

    Jesus says in Mark 11:24-25 *"Therefore I tell you, whatever you asked for in prayer, believe that you have received it, and it will be yours. And when you stand praying, if you hold anything against anyone, forgive him, so that your Father in heaven may forgive you your sins."*

- There will be times when God shows you things only for your benefit. There were times when God allowed me to discern or see something and I would begin sharing it with others. No one would believe me. I was confused because I know it was God who had revealed things to me. God responded one day to my prayer saying, "I never told you to tell anyone. I revealed those things to you so that you would pray." Ever noticed someone resisting you when you would share a word? There's resistance because they are not ready for what you have to say. Pray first. Wait on the Lord to instruct you when to share…and that's if you ever to share. God may send someone else to share the word. Maybe your job is to pray for the understanding of that person. Take it from me. Before you share what you have discerned or seen…pray.

    - It is NOT about your feelings. Discernment and seeing is not about you. It's about God. Be careful not to operate in your flesh. Discernment and seeing supernaturally is based on the Word of the Lord. This is not a time to gossip, sharing your opinions, or based upon your feelings. This is about God. He is choosing to use you.

    - Be sure to be led by the Holy Spirit. Several years ago, when I worked for an international women's ministry, we did a piece around a sailboat. I'll explain it here as I believe a sail might best illustrate the move of the Holy Spirit.

A sail is literally just a piece of canvas hoisted and then extended into the wind in such a way as to receive its full force. When you think of prayer that is self-guided it should remind you of a boat that labors with a person trying to move it by using an oar.

Can you imagine – a sailboat with a perfectly designed sail and the wind perfectly in place for the course? Though instead of the sail being raised and enjoying the excitement of journey – instead the sailor – chooses to get out the oars. The experience completely changes! What was once intended to produce joy has been replaced by labor. This really illustrates the difference between Spirit Guided discernment and prayer and Self-Guided fleshly discernment and prayer.

Our time with God – silent and seeking His face, operating in a spirit of discernment, waiting upon Him, is like becoming the canvas for God's Spirit to move us. We are powerless vessels similar to a boat without a sail. It cannot move toward its destination; it doesn't fulfill the journey that it was created for.

How do we know confidently that the Lord, through His Holy Spirit, is guiding us? Just as we know that wind cannot be seen, we recognize its movement, therefore, we must trust in the spirit of discernment and trust what He shows us.

When operating in spiritual discernment, we want to make sure we are not in our flesh, self-guiding what we think we discern or see. We do not want to claim God's name on a word or action that never came from Him. Therefore, we surrender and live by faith trusting in His promise to be guided by the Holy Spirit. There, He can make known His truth. It's up to us individually to be obedient to His instructions.

"Then you will call upon me and come and pray to me, and I will listen to you."
"You will seek me and find me when you seek me with all your heart."
Jeremiah 29:12-13

# PUT. PRAYER. INTO PRACTICE.
# A MONTH OF INTENTIONAL PRAYER.

Let's Pray! It's up to you if you want to fast and pray, but at least…let's pray.

## Protection

Let's pray a prayer of protection. God cover all of Your children as we go about doing what You have called us to do in this season. May a hedge of Your grace, power, and love surround us this day and every day especially as we move into a time of 31-days of prayer. In the name of Jesus. Amen.

**DAY 1**

## DAY 2

### Cancer

Pray for every person you know who has breast cancer, has survived breast cancer, has victory over breast cancer.

Call out each name aloud and spend today praying for them. Pray that all their bills (medical and household) are paid in full. Pray for their health. Pray their strength and pray over their immune system as they may have radiation or chemotherapy treatments. Pray their comfort and peace.

Praise God for every person who is or will soon to be victorious! Declare and decree their victory.

## Mental / Emotional Wounds

Ask God how to pray and be obedient to His instructions.

Pray for those who have been mentally and emotionally wounded or dealing with past rejection. Pray for their healing. Pray that their past wounds will not hinder the life God has ordained for them, but push them into their destiny. Pray they will not block or unintentionally abuse authentic relationships that God has sent their way to journey with them. Declare and decree an impartation of hope, joy, God's power and strength, and a fresh anointing.

**DAY 3**

## DAY 4

### Marriage

It's a day of praying for marriages. If your single, you can still pray by praying for those individuals who are married in your family, workplace, neighborhood or family. Let's pray...Pray for your marriage/spouse. Ask God to bless your marriage/spouse. Pray and ask God to reign down a fresh anointing upon your marriage/spouse today. Pray...Lord, break any heavy yoke that may be trying to attach itself or consume my spouse. Pray...Lord, may my spouse sense Your presence in every conversation they have today and everyone they come into contact with today. Pray...Lord, if there's anyone who tries to trick, trap, or cause them any harm or if any unholy person who has an assignment against my spouse we cancel the assignment of the enemy right now in the name of Jesus. Pray...Lord, place a strong hedge of protection around my marriage/spouse today. Pray... No weapon formed against my marriage/spouse and shall prosper. God, cause my spouse to think thoughts of You today and remind them how You joined us together. May we be intentional in our passionate interactions with one another today. Pray...Lord, may my spouse walk in godly authority, integrity and live a godly reputation. Lord, order their steps today. Lord, protect our eye gate and ear gate from any seductive, lustful, and Jezebel spirits. Cancel the assignment of the enemy. Block any ungodly temptation today. Lord, give my spouse favor today, and at the end of today when we connect after our long day, may we reflect on how we represented you today and reveal to us areas where we need to do better. In the name of Jesus I pray. Amen.

## Stewardship

Let's pray intentionally to become better stewards of finances. Make this prayer a prayer you pray for yourself and your finances. Place your hands over your wallet, dollar bills, or changes and begin by praying...God, I desire to become a consistent sower/philanthropist and invest in my children and leave a legacy. (If you do not have children change that line to invest in (students, children needing adopted, babies in the NICU, children in your neighborhood etc.) Pray that you will be a regular giver within your local church and one or two causes within your local community. Pray for a job/career and or small business profits to pay off your debts. Pray and ask God to show you how to use what He has given you financially in everyday living. Pray and ask God to show you how and where you have been wasteful and to show you how to cut costs. Pray, Lord give us this day our daily bread. Finally, pray and ask God to bless you financially and allow you to experience a overflow of financial outpouring. Amen!

## DAY 6

### Health and Wholeness

Do you want to be well? (John 5:6-9)

As Jesus asked the man by the pool of Bethesda. The man replied with an excuse. Today let's pray for health and wholeness without giving an excuse. Pray, Lord, I choose to be well. Pray that you will be obedient to the voice of the Lord in all things. Pray, Lord, I freely give you my mind...use it, transform it, adjust it, heal it. Pray for self-care. Pray for your mental and emotional capacity. Pray and ask God who in your circle needs to be released. For your physical well-being: Pray as you take medication. Pray before you eat. Pray for movement and exercise without accident. Pray for motivation to be well. Pray that you will follow God's plans and not your flesh. Pray that you will have strength when God calls you to give up sugary foods and when God calls you to exercise. Pray for a healthy mindset. Pray to be whole: Pray for revelation knowledge as you spend time in His word. Declare and decree to yourself to rise up and walk as God calls you forward.

## Joyful

**DAY 7**

Let's choose joy today! Lord, I choose to live joy and let that be my experience throughout today. Oh Lord, thank You for anointing me to bring good news to everyone I encounter today especially those who are afflicted. (Isaiah 61) Pray...Oh Lord, may my own grief be turned into joy. (John 16) Pray Psalm 51:12 Restore to me the joy of Your salvation And sustain me with a willing spirit. Pray...Lord, the moment grief, heaviness, darkness tries to strike, may I intentionally choose joy, dancing, and lean into the beauty of Your holiness and embrace Your Shekinah (Hebrew word meaning dwelling) Glory. Yes, Lord. I choose to dwell in Your promises and bask in Your glory. In the name of a Jesus I pray. Amen!

# DAY 8

## Heaviness Broken

Today we will be intentional about breaking heaviness that lurks around waiting to ambush someone's day, atmosphere, and or personal space. Pray...

Lord, I speak peace and comfort in my life, my neighbor's life, my co-worker's life, and in the life of my friends and families today. I pray for everyone around me who may be in a place of grieving to experience their heaviness dissipate. Lord, help me (help us) to breathe and release anything that has tried to create bondage. May we be intentional today to relax our shoulders, lift our heads, and walk with a boldness of Christ Jesus while living today in complete confidence that You are Lord. Father God, break the darkness, and let Your light shine through every area of my life. Yes! I permit You to shine Your light on those hidden things in my life that I must deal with to become free of heaviness. In the name of Jesus. Amen!

## Cast Out Fear

Pray...The Psalm of David. The LORD is my light and my salvation; whom shall I fear? the LORD is the strength of my life; of whom shall I be afraid? (Psalm 27:1 KJV)

Intentionally speak to yourself and declare and decree, "I will not have fear or be afraid." Declare and believe, "I have the strength of the LORD."

Pray, "In the name of Jesus, I will not be tormented by fear nor shall I be paralyzed by fear."

Declare and decree, "I can do all things through Christ who gives me strength...TODAY!"

Lord, thank you for equipping me with the full armor of God. I will walk in authority today without fear or trembling. I'm here to please You with my life according to the word of the Lord. In the name of Jesus. Amen.

**DAY 9**

# DAY 10

## Rest

Psalm 91:1 reads, "Whoever dwells in the shelter of the Most High will rest in the shadow of the Almighty."

Quick lesson before we pray.

Google defines '*dwell*' as:
1. verb: to live in or at a specified place
2. technical: a slight regular pause in the motion

Google defines '*rest*' as:
1. verb: cease work or movement in order to relax, refresh oneself, or recover strength.
2. noun: an instance or period of relaxing or ceasing to engage in strenuous or stressful activity.

Let's pray.
Lord, thank You for this word of rest. I make the choice today to live continuously in your presence where I will find rest. Father, throughout my day, I will be intentional to pause and reflect on the goodness of Jesus. Yes, God…I surrender and will slow down and see the beauty of everything around me. Even in times of trouble I will pause and see Your hand upon me… hiding me under Your shadow. Lord, help me to be intentional with my self-care so that I may take moments to be refreshed and revived under the shadow of the Almighty God. Father, thank You for this place of shelter from stress, worry, anxiety, and busyness. Satan comes to steal, kill, and destroy, but God I know You come to give life in abundance. I choose life, therefore, I choose to rest, dwell, pause, and be renewed. I speak rest. I declare and decree rest today in the name of Jesus. Amen.

## Faith

James 1:2-3 says, "Consider it pure joy, my brothers and sisters, whenever you face trials of many kinds, because you know that the testing of your faith produces perseverance." (NIV)

Today we choose faith. Let's pray.

Father, thank You!
God, I step into this day intentionally exercising my faith in all things. I speak faith to everyone in my circle of influence. Lord, I will share my faith with everyone I come into contact with today trusting that if they are not a follower of Jesus they will be by the time I have shared my testimony. Lord, I'm walking boldly in my faith today regardless of my circumstance…I choose to be obedient to Your instructions and remain faithful in all things. I declare and decree that I will exercise my faith despite difficulty. I declare and decree that I will walk by faith and not by sight. God, thank You for revealing to me that today is going to be a great day. I am counting today pure joy as I live the rest of my life by faith! Amen!

DAY 11

## DAY 12

### Purpose

"And we know that in all things God works for the good of those who love him, who have been called according to his purpose." (Romans 8:28)

Lord, what is it that you have purposed for Your children today and in the days to come? God, we know that we have the victory, and in this particular season how shall we live and move forward? Yes, I know that all things work together for the good of those who love You, and God the rest of the scripture says, "according to His (meaning Your) purpose." Lord, I choose to be intentional and live in my purpose. Help all of Your children identify what that is for each of us individually and collectively. I declare and I decree that I will walk in what You have purposed for me. I surrender. Lord, I'm available to You! Use me according to what You have purposed for me. In Jesus name... Amen!

## Increase

**DAY 13**

Lord, it's easy for us to petition for financial increase, but as I mature, I realize I need to adjust my prayer language to pray for an increase in wisdom and knowledge of You.

God increase my desire to be with You as a deer pants for water, I want to long for you. (Psalm 42:1)

Colossians 1:10 says, "that you may walk worthy of the Lord, fully pleasing Him, being fruitful in every good work and increasing in the knowledge of God;" (NKJV) This is what I long for as I grow in my walk with You.

Father, I want to be intentional and fully please You. God, I desire to bear fruit...be fruitful as I share the gospel and represent Jesus. I no longer want to walk in my fleshly desires and live based on how I feel. Lord, I choose to honor You in spirit and in truth surrendering my will to Yours.

Lord, use me to speak wisdom and knowledge to everyone I encounter today. Bless me with boldness, confidence, and maturity. God today, I am intentionally praying for increase. I pray for more of You in my life that will purposefully push out me and my stuff. May You, Lord, increase as I decrease. In the name of Jesus. Amen!

## DAY 14

### Lament

Lord, today we lament.

God, many of Your sons and daughters are fed up. Killings. Murders of innocent Black and brown people from those who are called to protect. Homelessness. Government scandals. Division. Human Trafficking. Domestic Violence. Job loss. Divorce. Financial lack. Debt that is paralyzing. Deaths. Cancer. Loss. Marginalized people. Injustices. Children in cages. Broken systems. Disproportion of wealth. Do I/we go on, Lord? Father, I/we just need to lament today.

God, You sit on the throne. Don't You see us? Do You see what's going on? We are exhausted. It's becoming the norm to read headlines day after day with a different name inserted that there's yet another killing of an innocent life.

God, if I am to pray an authentic prayer…I must ask, "Where are You?"

Please Lord, hear and answer our prayers. We are tired of the ongoing narratives that are painting an untrue image of the disadvantaged people . God, expose those things that are hidden.

Lord, don't You see our faithfulness? Your word says that You will honor those of us who honor You (1 Samuel 2:30). Oh Lord, save us!

We sow seeds to build the kingdom. We pray. We fast. And today we lament.

Yet, I/we love You! We know You are present. So we wait for the manifestation of Your glory at the appointed time. God, we know You already know that we are barely holding on, and we cry out asking, "God, let us breathe. Let us come up for air." God, we need a break from all of the chaos and uncertainties.

Lord, please hear our prayers. Breathe life into Your children. We weep!

God…(continue to lament before God and pour out your heart). He can handle our time of lament.

## Unity

In the name of Jesus. Amen.

Father, today I intentionally pray for unity. Lord, I ask that You will infuse me with Your abiding love for all people, regardless of their race, demographic, background, their religion, or differences that may challenge me to want to insert my prejudice when You have created us as unique people. Lord, may we come to an understanding that beauty is that none of us are the same. God, help me to embrace that we are all Your creation and You desire that all be saved. Use me today to share my faith with those not like me and help me disciple someone that is not in my community. Lord, send someone who is not like me to disciple me in my walk with Christ. Lord, bring us together in spirit and in truth. I pray that You will give me the wisdom and knowledge to build authentic relationships across cultural groups. May I display unconditional love always. In the name of Jesus. Amen

**DAY 15**

## DAY 16

### Available

"Lord, I'm available to You.
My will I give to You
I'll do what You say do
Use me Lord to show someone the way
and enable me to say
My storage is empty and I am available to You."

(Song by Milton Brunson and the Thompson Community Singers)

May this be our intentional prayer today. Lord, I am available. Lord, not my will but thy will be done. Lord, I'll do whatever You instruct me to do. Lord, use me to help someone else. Lord, I open my mouth and declare, "I'm empty. I am available to You." Here I am Lord. Use me. I surrender. Amen.

## DAY 17

### Oil

Lord, I pray that Your oil will drench me today. May it flow throughout every fabric of my being. Saturate me with a fresh anointing that moves me to rest, pray, have clarity, and causes a revival within me and with everyone I come into contact. Lord, may we experience a supernatural encounter today.

"You prepare a table before me in the presence of my enemies. You anoint my head with oil; my cup overflows." Psalm 23:5

Note: if you have anointing oil (pray over some oil) anoint your head. Now pray, Lord, may my cup overflow today. Amen!

## DAY 18

### Release

Lord, today I'm praying a prayer of release. Lord, I release myself from self-imposed bondage. Lord, I also release anyone that I have not forgiven and today I forgive them. Lord, today I also release myself from guilt and shame that I may be holding onto. Lord, today I intentionally remove the chains and walk in freedom.

Father, as I pray today, help me to let go of resentment towards others. Lord, may others let go of resentment. May all of Your children decide today to release whatever bondage we may be holding onto that is weighing us down, suffocating us, and or paralyzing us, and keeping us from living the abundant life You promised us. May we be released from the prisons we willingly allowed ourselves to enter.

In the Name of Jesus and with the Holy Spirit's power, I choose to release myself of all unhealthy bitterness, rage, anger, gossip, along with every form of malice. I chose to receive and to not miss Your grace for I know whom the Son has set free is free indeed. I declare that I have been released today and I will release others for what I have held against them. Amen.

## Blessing

**DAY 19**

Lord, bless me and bless everyone I lift in prayer today. Heavenly Father, today I intentionally pray with a grateful heart and lift name after name unto You asking that You would bless them. Lord, I pray that You bless me with divine healing in every area of my life, (mind, body, spirit, will, emotions and physical being). Lord, don't stop with me, but bless (insert names). Give each person I have prayed for today Your divine healing, blessing, plan, and revelation knowledge. Lord, bless all of Your sons and daughters with health, wholeness, and financial wealth in the name of Jesus Christ. Lord, I walk in boldness today and ask You to expand my territory so I may continue to do what You've called me to do. Lord, please replace my ashes for beauty, my mourning with the oil of joy, the spirit of heaviness in my life with the garment of praise: may I be a tree of righteousness planted of the Lord. God, may You be glorified today! And Lord, I ask that You give unto me the manifestation of every blessing, miracle, and every healing You have for me, and the manifestation of divine blessing, divine healing, divine financial wealth, and divine health upon me and on the inside of me today. This I pray in the name of Jesus. Amen!

## DAY 20

### Success

Lord, grant us success today.

Father, in Psalm 118:25 we read these words, "Lord, save us! Lord, grant us success!"

This is our prayer today.

Lord, we are intentionally praying scripture as we ask You to save us and grant us success. Today.

In the name of Jesus. Amen.

## Repent

**DAY 21**

"Repent, then, and turn to God, so that your sins may be wiped out, that times of refreshing may come from the Lord." Acts 3:19 NIV

God, I repent. Lord, I choose to take a step of growth and maturity and turn from those things I know are not from You. Today, I intentionally let go of my pride and living in my flesh thinking "I have no sin." I have sinned and for that I repent. Lord Jesus, thank you for wiping my sins away and allowing Your refreshing to spill out all over me. Lord, may I experience new mercies every morning. Great is Your faithfulness. (Lamentations 3:23).

Search us, O God, and know our hearts today; try us and see if there be some wicked way in us; cleanse us from every sin and set us free according to Your Will. (Psalm 139) In the name of Jesus. Amen.

Adding to today's (Day 21) intentional prayer.
Let's end the day praying, declaring, and decreeing, "It Is Well."

https://music.apple.com/us/album/it-is-well-with-my-soul/1073482443?i=1073482565&fbclid=IwAR3k9SIOUiypYiiwPcNKg467nzW8tafUDvO_hOObXLaTnaIZN9UEMaMGPrM

# DAY 22

## Love

God, teach me to love. That's my prayer today.

Mark 12:30-31 says, "Love the Lord your God with all your heart and with all your soul and with all your mind and with all your strength." The second is this: 'Love your neighbor as yourself.' There is no commandment greater than these."

Heavenly Father, help me. Today I intentionally pray to love You with every fiber of my being (Mind, body, soul, strength). God, I desire a relationship with You and choose to pray, be still, listen, and study Your word. I want to authentically love You. I want to know You and the power of Your resurrection. (Philippians 3:10)

Lord, teach me how to love myself. I realize I haven't been able to truly love my neighbor because I haven't taken the time to love myself. Help me today. Help me see my truth which is the love of God transforming me with every breath I take. Lord, help me to pause and breathe in Your love and breathe out any and everything that contradicts that truth. May my heartbeat line up with Yours and may love abound today. I declare and decree that Your love will cast out lies and fear that have been holding me hostage. Today, I declare that I am free to love. In the name of Jesus. Amen.

## Peace

Lord, You are my peace. May Your peace consume the earth today, and may Your sons and daughters experience peace which passes all understanding. Cancel anxiety. Shut out all the noise. Quiet every distraction. Father, may we hear Your still small voice today. May we recognize Your presence today. God, we pray for a hush and a calming across the land. Lord, as we pray for and seek peace today, may we hear the birds chirping, see the colors of the leaves, breathe in Your sweet smelling fragrance, witness the beauty of Your holiness. May we experience an overwhelming sense of Your peace today. Father God, when we speak, may it flow like a feather falling from the sky. May we speak at a whisper and feel the slowness... the comfort of Your loving arms wrapped around us as we rest in Your peace today. May all hurrying, confusion, wrestling, anxiety, stress, people pleasing...come to a halt where we find peace today. Amen.

I hear God saying, "Hush..."

"Peace I leave with you; my peace I give you. I do not give to you as the world gives.
Do not let your hearts be troubled and do not be afraid."
John 14:27

**DAY 23**

## See

"Immediately, something like scales fell from Saul's eyes, and he could see again. He got up and was baptized," Acts 9:18 NIV

Lord, I want to see. Please remove the scales from my eyes so I can see. Right now I see things that I am misinterpreting. Right now things appear unsure and foggy. Lord, what I see, I'm seeing through fleshly lens. Lord, I want to see with clarity. Lord, I ask to see supernaturally and so I may pray according to Your desires. Lord, I desire the scales be removed from my eyes so I can respond to what You are calling me to do. Right now I'm distracted by my lack of having the ability to see because of all the untruths and unholy things I have previously focused on.

I hear You calling me to come higher! Please Lord remove these scales from my eyes so I can see!

"Look among the nations! Observe! Be astonished! Wonder! Because I am doing something in your days-- You would not believe if you were told." Habakkuk 1:5 NAS

"The LORD said to Abram, after Lot had separated from him, "Now lift up your eyes and look from the place where you are, northward and southward and eastward and westward;" Genesis 13:14 NAS

Oh yes! Now, I see.
I see blessings. I see hope. I see healing.
I see truth. I see reconciliation. I see love.
I see Jesus.
I see abundant life. I see...

What will you do, now that you see?

## Prosper

Lord, I pray that all of Your children will prosper. Thank You for 3 John 1:2 that says, "Beloved, I pray that you may prosper in all things and be in health, just as your soul prospers."

May this day be filled with prosperity. Financial. Health. Wisdom. Love. Knowledge. Life. Business. Not just for me Lord, but for every person I see today, every name I lift today, and every man, woman, boy and girl who professes You are Lord. Amen!

"Jesus said to him, "If you can believe, all things are possible to him who believes." Immediately the father of the child cried out and said with tears, "Lord, I believe; help my unbelief!" Mark 9:23-24 NKJV

**DAY 25**

## DAY 26

### Unbelief

Lord, I believe, but help my unbelief. God, I want to believe even in those times and seasons when things don't look as if they will turn out good. Father, help me keep my eyes on You and trust that You know what's best.

I choose to live by faith and believe in You and not in my fleshy wishful thinking. I realize being wishful is not belief. Lord, I'm giving up being on the fence. Today I make the choice to let go and rest fully in Your will...not mine.

I declare and decree that doubt is canceled right now in the name of Jesus. Lord, touch my mind and transform it. Cancel the lies and torture of the enemy.

Lord, I cry out to You, "I believe. Help my unbelief." In the name of Jesus. Amen.

## Whatever

*"Whatever you have learned or received or heard from me, or seen in me—put it into practice. And the God of peace will be with you."* Philippians 4:9 NIV

**DAY 27**

"Finally, brothers and sisters, whatever is true, whatever is noble, whatever is right, whatever is pure, whatever is lovely, whatever is admirable—if anything is excellent or praiseworthy—think about such things." Philippians 4:8 NIV

God, I pray that I will live in the "whatever" lane today and always. Whatever is true. Whatever is noble. Whatever is right. Whatever is pure. Whatever is lovely. Whatever is admirable. Whatever is excellent. Whatever is praiseworthy. Lord, I intentionally choose to live in Your truth of whatever is…

God, breathe on Your people today. Transform our thinking and allow us to fully experience the "whatever" Your servant Paul shared with us in the Bible. I pray that the weight of life would melt from our shoulders as we take Your yoke upon us and learn of You. Lord, I surrender my burden and receive Your yoke so that I can find rest for my soul. Lord, I choose to walk in the words Paul shares in Philippians 4, and may I live in the "whatever." In the name of Jesus. Amen!

**Prayer** *In Motion*

# DAY 28

## Live

Dear God, there are days when Your sons and daughters are struggling and walking around hopelessly confused and appear to be defeated. There are times when we think it's our last day here on earth. Lord, regardless of what may be coming at me, I declare that I shall not die, but live, and declare the works of the Lord.

"I shall not die, but live, And declare the works of the Lord." Psalm 118:17 NKJV

Lord, I declare and decree, "This is the day that the Lord has made. I will rejoice and be glad in it." (Psalm 118:24 NLT)

Today, I stop waddling and saying woe is me. Today, I rise. Today, is a day that I am grateful. Thank You, God! Today, I will be intentional and live. I will display the goodness of the Lord. In the name of Jesus. Amen.

## Abundant

Today I declare life more abundantly.

"The thief does not come except to steal, and to kill, and to destroy. I have come that they may have life, and that they may have it more abundantly." John 10:10 NKJV

Lord, I'm being intentional today. It does not matter the circumstance I may be facing. All I know is that I'm holding onto Your Word. You came so I can have life and have it more abundantly. Today will be a day I live in abundance. Tomorrow as well! In the name of Jesus. I choose to live! AMEN!

**DAY 29**

## DAY 30

### Prophecy

Read Deuteronomy 28:3-14 and prophesy over yourself.

Teaching moment: Pray Scriptures. Pray God's Word back to Him.

Lord, thank You for blessing me in the city and in the country. Thank You for blessing me when I come and go. Thank You Lord for granting that the enemies who rise up against me will be defeated before me. They will come at me from one direction but flee from me in seven. Lord, thank You for sending a blessing on my home, property, business, and on everything I put my hand to. Lord, thank You for blessing me in the land You are giving me. Lord, thank You for granting me abundant prosperity. I praise You Jesus for opening the heavens, the storehouse of my bounty, to send rain on my land in season and to bless all the work of my hands. God, I declare and decree that I will lend to many nations but will borrow from none. God, thank you for making me the head, not the tail. I surrender as I pay attention to the commands of the Lord my God. Father, I will not turn aside from any of the commands You give me today, to the right or to the left, following other gods and serving them. I choose today to walk in obedience to You.

"The tongue has the power of life and death, and those who love it will eat its fruit."
Proverbs 18:21 NIV

Today, I prophesy to myself and speaking life and not death, and will be obedient to the commands of the Lord. In the name of Jesus. Amen!

## Pray

**DAY 31**

"After this manner therefore pray ye: Our Father which art in heaven, Hallowed be thy name. Thy kingdom come, Thy will be done in earth, as it is in heaven. Give us this day our daily bread. And forgive us our debts, as we forgive our debtors. And lead us not into temptation, but deliver us from evil: For thine is the kingdom, and the power, and the glory, for ever. Amen." Matthew 6:9-13 KJV

# PUT. PRAYER. INTO PRACTICE. AND REPEAT...

Although we are at the conclusion of our 31 days together, I urge you to continue to pray, fast and seek the Lord for every area of your life.

DAY 3

# PRAYING POSITIONS

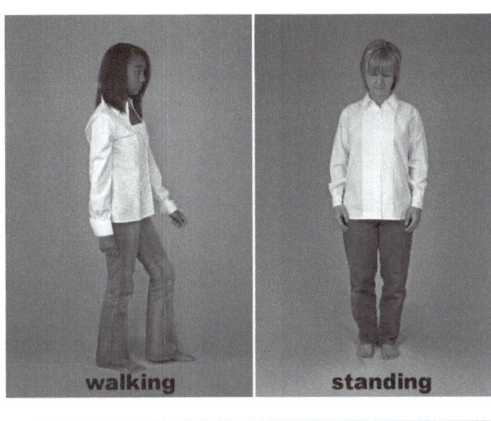

walking | standing

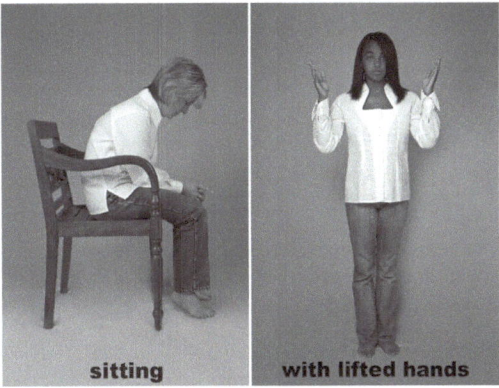

sitting | with lifted hands

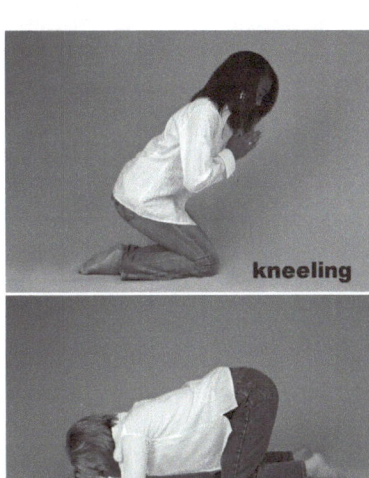

kneeling

bowing

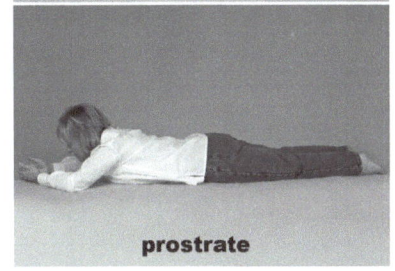

prostrate

# PRAYING POSITIONS

**(excerpt from *Ready to Pray* by Gail Dudley)**

**Kneeling,** head bowed, hands folded
(I Kings 8:54; Ezra 9:5; Luke 22:41; Acts 9:40)

**Bowing,** head to the ground, hands face down on the ground next to head
(Exod. 34:8; Neh. 8:6; Psalm 72:11)

**Laying flat,** on the floor, face down, with hands stretched out (*prostrate*)
(Joshua 7:6; Ezra 10:1; Matt. 26:39; Mark 14:35)

**Slow, leisurely walking,** eyes open (walking)
(2 Kings 4:35)

**Standing,** head slightly bowed, facing the altar
(Neh. 9:5; Mark 11:25; Luke 18:13)

**Sitting,** head bowed, leaning forward, eyes closed, hands folded
(1 Chron. 17:16-27)

**With lifted hands,** hands raised and spread, palms up, eyes looking upward
(2 Chron. 6:12, 13; Psalm 63:4; 1 Tim. 2:8)

# Guide for Organizing a Prayer Advance

*Prayer in Motion* is a time to seek the face and heart of God on behalf of our communities. It is not a time to seek His hand or His blessing. The desire is meet Him and to intercede and stand in the gap expressing the need for God's grace to be bestowed upon others. Encourage people in and around your communities to come together for one hour, four hours, eight hours, and or two or three days to pray.

Let us call to Jesus so that He may lead and guide us as we reach out to the individuals who are marginalized, lonely, lost, hurt, seeking, facing oppression, lack, but wanting to be revived, delivered, and engaged in biblical teaching of the truth. Let us pray for a worldwide prayer movement, presidents around the world, government, businesses, families, marriages, students and health and wealth. It is time to bring individuals together on one accord as we seek God's face and experience a mighty move of His power that can bring about transformation.

## Prayer Advance Implementation:

- Pray and ask God for direction.
- Get a team of volunteers to serve in the roles of administration, intercessors, hosting locations, etc.
- Determine the date(s) for the prayer gathering.
- Share the theme Prayer in Motion using the scripture "Call To Me" Jer. 33:3
- Determine the timeframe for intercession.
- Ask for team coordinators to coordinate teams in each community and be sure to involve churches.
- Have a system in place in order to keep track of all prayer requests, e-mails, and team coordinators.
- Organize outreach efforts.
- Utilize social media to share announcements about the prayer gathering.
- Fast and pray.

# Prayer Models

There are many ways of coming together to pray on behalf of others during a prayer advance that will help maintain the enthusiasm of those who are participating. Listed below are four models of community prayer you might like to introduce to your team:

1. **Small Groups**

    The team leader of each prayer gathering brings together a team to pray over the cause/need. Each team leader would send out an announcement to invite the community, neighborhood, or subdivision for a time of prayer. The announcement could read something like this: "We invite you to join our time of prayer on (date). Would you please consider joining our group to pray during this prayer gathering?"

    Include additional information such as the location and time. You may also include suggested materials or requests for prayer as well. Materials could include: water, Bible, pen, paper, journal, etc.

    The team leader determines the outline for the time of prayer. The team leader may decide to have 5, 7 or 12 intercessors each to pray for one hour or you may decide to have the entire team pray collectively for 3, 7, 12 or 24 hours, etc.

2. **Acts 4**

    This may be in a church, house, or in a park, etc. Acts 4 involves everyone praying aloud at the same time, as modeled in Acts 4:24. The leader, having introduced the cause/need to be prayed, will direct those present to pray in this way. Some people may decide to pray silently during this time of prayer. That's not a problem. The purpose is to have everyone praying.

3. **Walk and Pray**

    You may decide to have a team of individuals walking and praying during the prayer gathering. The team leader will share the prayer requests of the community in which the team will walk and pray. The group may decide to walk and pray together or split up and take different areas of the community to ensure that every area is covered in prayer.

4. **Silent Prayer**

    As a contrast to the above models, silence can be very effective at a prayer gathering. One may find the need to sit and read scriptures during the time of prayer: Inserting names of individuals throughout the scriptures in place of "Me" and "You."

## Suggested Books on prayer

*A Hunger for God* by John Piper, (Crossway Books & Bibles)
*A Journey to Victorious Praying* by Bill Thrasher, (Moody Publishers)
*Beyond the Veil* by Alice Smith, (Renew Books)
*Developing a Prayer-Care-Share Lifestyle*, (HOPE Ministries)
*Disciple's Prayer Life* by T.W. Hunt & Catherine Walker
*Fervent* by Priscilla Shirer
*Fresh Wind, Fresh Fire* by Jim Cymbala, (Zondervan)
*How to Hear from God* by Joyce Meyer, (FaithWords)
*Intercessory Prayer* by Dutch Sheets, (Gospel Light)
*Intimacy with the Almighty* by Charles R. Swindoll, (Countryman)
*I Told the Mountain to Move* by Patricia Raybon, (SaltRiver)
*Learning to Pray Through the Psalms* by James W. Sire, (InterVarsity Press)
*Possessing the Gates of the Enemy* by Cindy Jacobs, (Chosen)
*Pray with Purpose, Live with Passion* by Debbie Williams, (Howard Books)
*Prayer: Finding the Heart's True Home* by Richard J. Foster (HarperOne)
*Prayer 101: Experiencing the Heart of God* by Warren Wiersbe (Cook Communications)
*Prayer Shield* by C. Peter Wagner, (Gospel Light)
*Prayers that Avail Much* by Germaine Copeland (World Ministries, Inc.)
*Praying God's Word* by Beth Moore, (Broadman & Holman Publishers)
*Praying with Women of the Bible* by Nancy Kennedy, (Zondervan)
*Ready to Pray* by Gail Dudley
*Spurgeon on Prayer & Spiritual Warfare*, by Charles Spurgeon, (Whitaker House)
*The Power of a Praying Woman* by Stormie Omartian, (Harvest House Publishers)
*What Happens When Women Pray* by Evelyn Christensen, (Cook Communications)

## Suggested Books on Fasting

*Fasting* by Jentezen Franklin, (Charisma House)
*The Daniel Fast*, by Susan Gregory, (Tyndale House)

# FOLLOW GAIL

 **Twitter:** @Gaildudley

 **Facebook:** www.facebook.com/GailSpeaks

 **Instagram:** @Gaildudley

 **LinkedIn:** linkedin.com/in/gaildudley

614.441.8178 | GED@MIMTODAY.ORG | WWW.GAILDUDLEY.COM

# "PRAYER IN MOTION..." REVIEWS

"For many years I prayed. My prayers went something like this, "Thank you, God, for everything. Forgive me for everything. Please help me with everything!" I joined an amazing church where we focus a lot on prayer and the power behind it. Learning and praying more, I have seen God work in so many different ways. The peace He gives me during a storm and learning to trust in Him when His answer is NO, and I want a YES have truly deepened my walk with GOD. Through my struggle, I decided to attend one of Gail's prayer seminars entitled Prayer in Motion. I sat there, amazed as she taught the class. Jesus shines through her. I was holding onto every word. She led us through section after section and step after step. Gail than encouraged us to get into one of seven prayer positions. She asked us to choose one in which we may be uncomfortable. She said pick a prayer position we do not usually find ourselves in. "Ok. I can do this," I said to myself. I bowed to Jesus, and I prayed fervently for my teenage daughter, who attended the seminar with me and was in a significant spiritual warfare. Gail closed the workshop in prayer, and I left holding on to every word. Leaning against the wall in the hallway was my daughter. She looked broken. I pulled out the tools Gail shared in Prayer in Motion and prayed with my daughter. We cried, and within a few minutes of Gail ending the seminar, my daughter received Jesus! Hallelujah! I highly recommend Gail's books, resources, articles, and workshops on prayer. I encourage this prayer manual Prayer in Motion. "Pray without ceasing." 1 Thessalonians 5:17. Gail has taught me that prayer does not end at amen, but it sets your prayer in motion!."

~ Nanda Grubb

> ## "NAIL YOUR FAITH TO THE WALL

*Gail Dudley's work with women has been a force in my life throughout the past year. Helping her bring God to the masses from the page has kept me upbeat and fighting even when it was darkest.*

*When you get that call "Tam, God laid it on my heart to release this book Now!" I'm thinking, "Okay". She sent the file and as I did my initial read through tears flowed. I needed the content in this book like dry land needs rain.*

*I did her edit and sent it back to her. She had no idea that I'd printed a copy and attached the pages to my wall. As guests come by, dozens of people have been inspired by her book before it's even published! To God Be The Glory!"*

~ Tam Jernigan,
*Editor, and Believer*

**THIS IS NOT A BOOK THAT WILL READ LIKE A STORY. IT IS A PRAYER MANUAL.**

It's a tool that you can use to guide you along your prayer journey. Pray long prayers? Short prayers? Lift up the name of Jesus when you are exhausted? *This manual is for you.*

Hosting a prayer summit, organizing prayer walks, or a missionary prayer journey? *This manual is for you.*

"*I was so blessed to hear Gail during her workshop Prayer in Motion*. When she announced the release of this manual, I was more than thrilled. I can keep this manual in my car, at home, throw it in my tote bag to pull out whenever I want to pray, write prayer requests, or have questions on prayer. *Through Gail's teaching and writing, I have learned that when we put prayer in motion, God can do immeasurable things*. I am always delighted to read Gail's books. I learn so much from them and her. Her books and writing always seem to come at the right time. I am currently using Urgent Plea for Prayer: 31-days of prayer with a group of women. We love it! Many of my prayers have been answered during this time. I'm learning how to pray with the tools she offers, along with believing God and waiting on Him. *Gail is an amazing woman of God who also fervently prays for her audience and will check in with us from time to time to see how we are doing*. If you are reading the back cover of this prayer manual, don't put it down. Buy two and gift one to someone else."

*Heather Cook, Fulton, IL*

*To contact Gail:*
GED@MIMToday.org
www.GailDudley.com

$24.97
ISBN 978-1-7336986-9-6

www.ingramcontent.com/pod-product-compliance
Lightning Source LLC
Chambersburg PA
CBHW042001150426
43194CB00002B/82